POWER PLAYS

THE NEXT 100 YEARS OF ENERGY

by Nikole Brooks Bethea

Raintree is an imprint of Capstone Global Library Limited, a company incorporated in England and Wales
having its registered office at 264 Banbury Road, Oxford, OX2 7DY Registered company number: 6695582

www.raintree.co.uk
myorders@raintree.co.uk

Edited by Mandy Robbins
Art Directed by Nathan Gassman
Designed by Ted Williams
Original illustrations © Capstone Global Library Limited 2017
Illustrated by Alan Brown
Coloured by Sara Foresti
Picture research by Jo Miller
Production by Katy LaVigne
Originated by Capstone Press
Printed and bound in China

ISBN 978 1 4747 1215 6
20 19 18 17 16
10 9 8 7 6 5 4 3 2 1

British Library Cataloguing in Publication Data
A full catalogue record for this book is available from
the British Library.

Acknowledgements
We would like to thank the following for permission to reproduce photographs: Design Element: Shutterstock:
pixelparticle (backgrounds)

Every effort has been made to contact copyright holders of material reproduced in this book. Any omissions
will be rectified in subsequent printings if notice is given to the publisher.

All the internet addresses (URLs) given in this book were valid at the time of going to press. However, due
to the dynamic nature of the Internet, some addresses may have changed, or sites may have changed or
ceased to exist since publication. While the author and publisher regret any inconvenience this may cause
readers, no responsibility for any such changes can be accepted by either the author or the publisher.

CONTENTS

ENERGY PAST AND PRESENT

Kami! Ken! It's great to have you visit.

Hi!

Hi, Aunt Luna!

Why is it so dark in here?

A storm knocked out the power earlier this morning.

Aw, man. I forgot to charge my phone before leaving home. Now it's dead, and I can't recharge it.

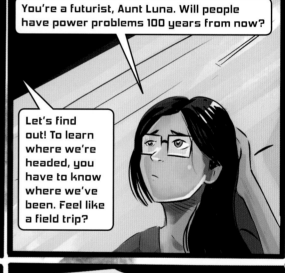

You're a futurist, Aunt Luna. Will people have power problems 100 years from now?

Let's find out! To learn where we're headed, you have to know where we've been. Feel like a field trip?

There's an agricultural museum a few miles away. It has a working farm like in the 1800s.

Why is there smoke coming from the chimney in the summer?

People cooked on wood-burning stoves long ago. There were no modern ovens. Wood was the fuel they used for cooking.

Welcome to the Tri-State power generating station, Luna. What brings you here today?

My niece and nephew would like to learn how electricity is made, Joe.

I'm the plant's mechanical engineer. I'll give you a tour.

Coal is the fuel here. It became important in the 1800s. Coal powered machines, steamships and railways.

It later fueled furnaces at steel manufacturing plants. By 1910 coal had overtaken wood as a main fuel source.

Today, making electricity starts when powdered coal is blown into the power plant's boiler. As the coal burns, water running through boiler tubes is turned to steam.

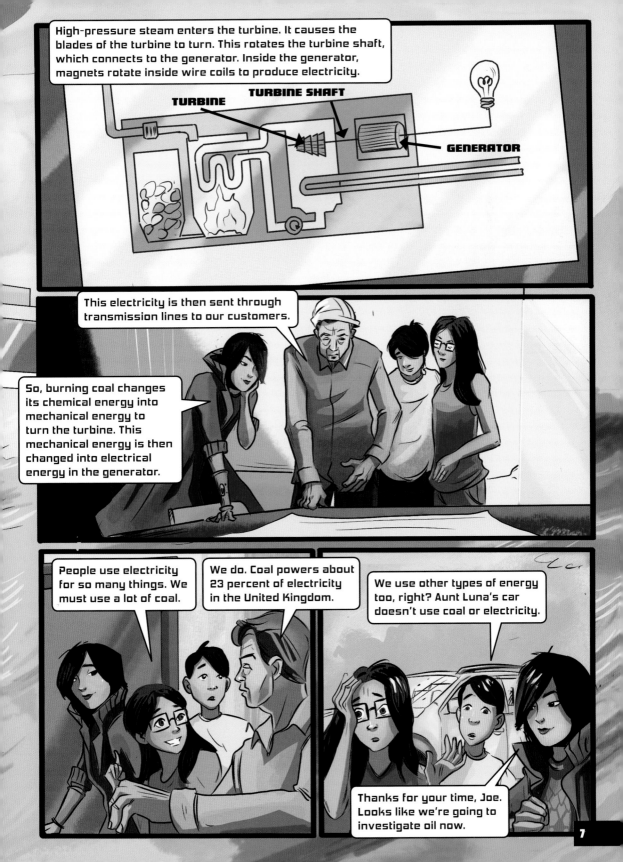

High-pressure steam enters the turbine. It causes the blades of the turbine to turn. This rotates the turbine shaft, which connects to the generator. Inside the generator, magnets rotate inside wire coils to produce electricity.

TURBINE SHAFT

TURBINE

GENERATOR

This electricity is then sent through transmission lines to our customers.

So, burning coal changes its chemical energy into mechanical energy to turn the turbine. This mechanical energy is then changed into electrical energy in the generator.

People use electricity for so many things. We must use a lot of coal.

We do. Coal powers about 23 percent of electricity in the United Kingdom.

We use other types of energy too, right? Aunt Luna's car doesn't use coal or electricity.

Thanks for your time, Joe. Looks like we're going to investigate oil now.

This place is huge! What is it?

It's an oil refinery. Crude oil is petroleum, which means "rock oil." Oil droplets are located in the pore spaces of rock underground. Oil is another fossil fuel.

Kids, this is Hillary. She's a chemical engineer. Hill, the kids were wondering about the fuel we use in vehicles.

Oh, oil! Oil wells pump oil from the ground. But it can't be used to power cars until it's refined.

Refining oil cleans it and separates it into parts. The parts are mixed to create different fuels and chemicals.

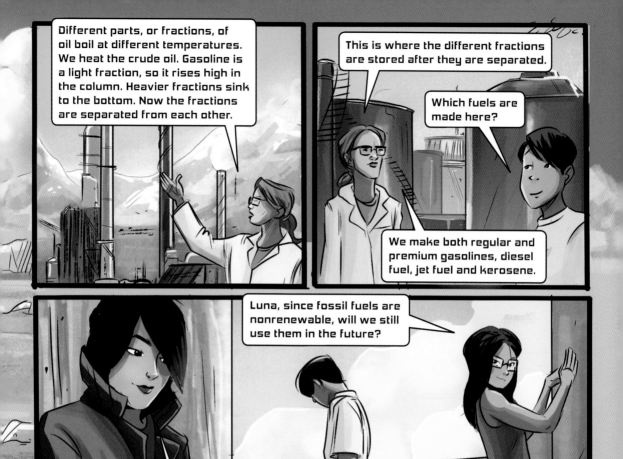

THE GREENHOUSE EFFECT ||||||||||||

When sunlight hits the Earth, some of its energy is absorbed, and some is reflected back to space. Earth's atmosphere has a natural layer of greenhouse gases that traps some of this heat. Burning fossil fuels adds extra greenhouse gases to the atmosphere. Most scientists think that these additional gases are trapping more heat than necessary. This is called global warming. Man-made global warming can cause extreme weather patterns and change sea levels. The results could be disastrous.

I'm Carter, the well field's geologist. Can I help you folks?

Yeah, we're wondering what natural gas is and why it could be the fuel of the future.

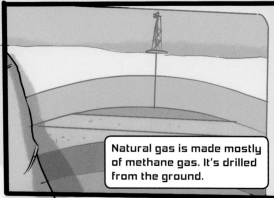

Natural gas is made mostly of methane gas. It's drilled from the ground.

We can access more natural gas by cracking the rock underground.

That's fracking, right? Isn't there a controversy about that?

Yes, but we're careful to avoid causing pollution and earthquakes.

But, Luna, don't we already use natural gas as an energy source in our present time?

Yes, but in 25 years cleaner-burning natural gas may replace coal as the main fuel at many power plants.

Will natural gas only be used in power plants in 25 years?

Definitely not. My vehicle is powered with natural gas. The emissions from natural gas vehicles are much cleaner. The use of natural gas as a transportation fuel has increased 10 percent in the last 25 years.

Interesting! Thanks, Carter!

This is a solar neighbourhood. All homes here generate some of their own electricity from these solar panels on the roofs.

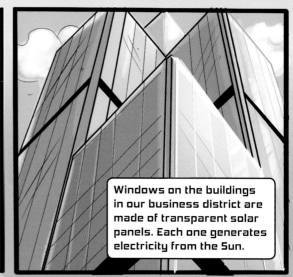

Windows on the buildings in our business district are made of transparent solar panels. Each one generates electricity from the Sun.

The car park and streets are made of solar panels, too. Of course, solar power is only generated when the parking spaces are vacant.

What do you do if snow covers the streets and car parks?

Heaters can be installed in the solar panels to melt snow.

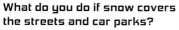

That's awesome!

Solar energy seems like the perfect clean energy source.

Well, it's not perfect. We always need a backup energy source for dark nights and cloudy days.

That makes sense. Thanks for the great information!

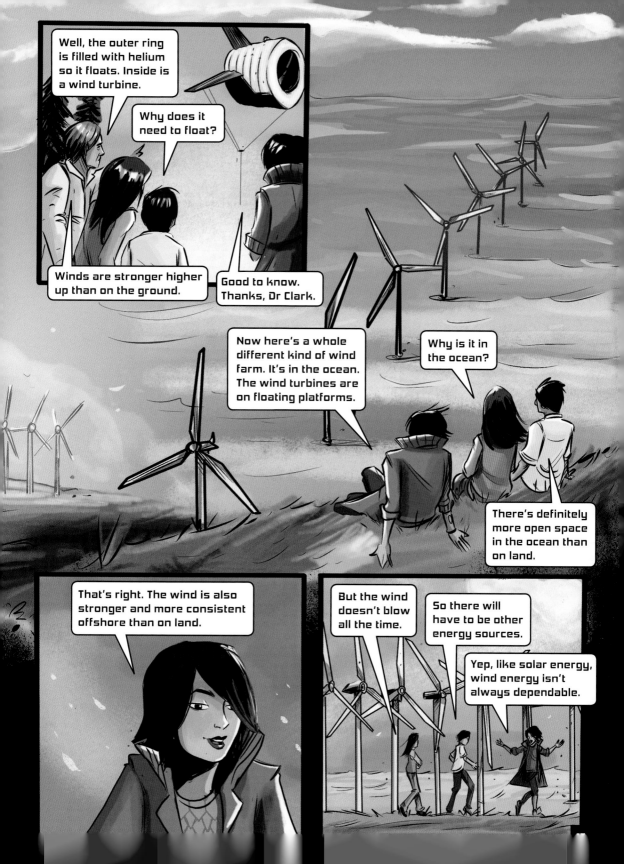

It looks like the power of the wind blowing over the ocean may be harnessed. But I wonder if we will be able to use the power of the ocean itself.

This looks like some sort of device using wave energy.

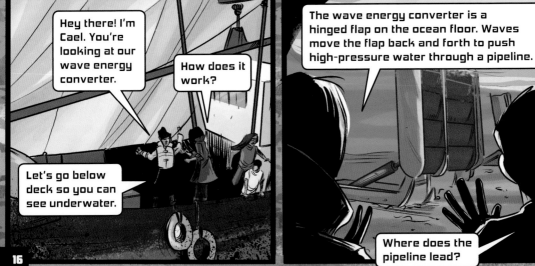

Hey there! I'm Cael. You're looking at our wave energy converter.

How does it work?

Let's go below deck so you can see underwater.

The wave energy converter is a hinged flap on the ocean floor. Waves move the flap back and forth to push high-pressure water through a pipeline.

Where does the pipeline lead?

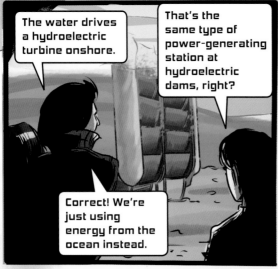

The water drives a hydroelectric turbine onshore.

That's the same type of power-generating station at hydroelectric dams, right?

Correct! We're just using energy from the ocean instead.

We have a wave farm too. It uses floating converters instead of submersible ones. Come on, I'll show you.

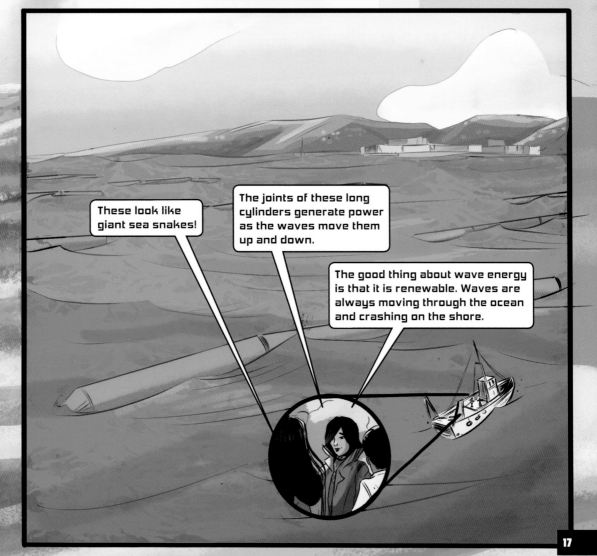

These look like giant sea snakes!

The joints of these long cylinders generate power as the waves move them up and down.

The good thing about wave energy is that it is renewable. Waves are always moving through the ocean and crashing on the shore.

Welcome to our photobioreactor. I'm Grace, the plant's microbiologist. These tubes grow algae for fuel.

Algae as fuel!?

Yep! In my time algae biofuel has replaced petroleum fuels. We use them in vehicles.

This algae-filled water is pumped through tubes. The tubes of algae are exposed to sunlight. Photosynthesis occurs within the tubes, and the algae grow.

These are experimental algae ponds. But weather conditions, temperature and sunlight can't be controlled like they are inside the facility.

I just don't see how you can get fuel from algae.

We harvest the algae and filter the water out. Next we squeeze out algae oil. Then we add a chemical that makes the algae release more oil.

So what's so great about using algae biofuels?

Algae is a renewable resource. It grows quickly. Biofuels have been made from corn and soybeans too, but using algae allows those crops to remain food crops.

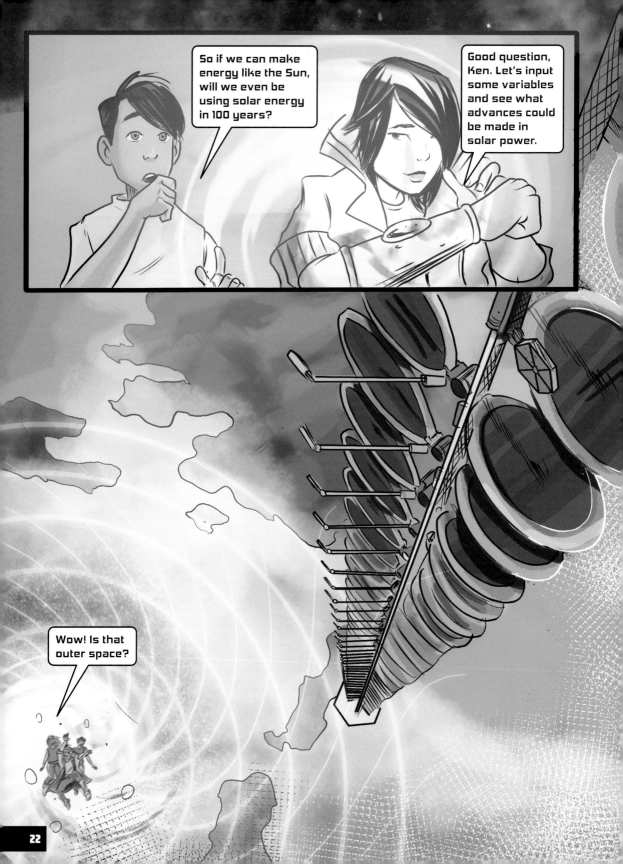

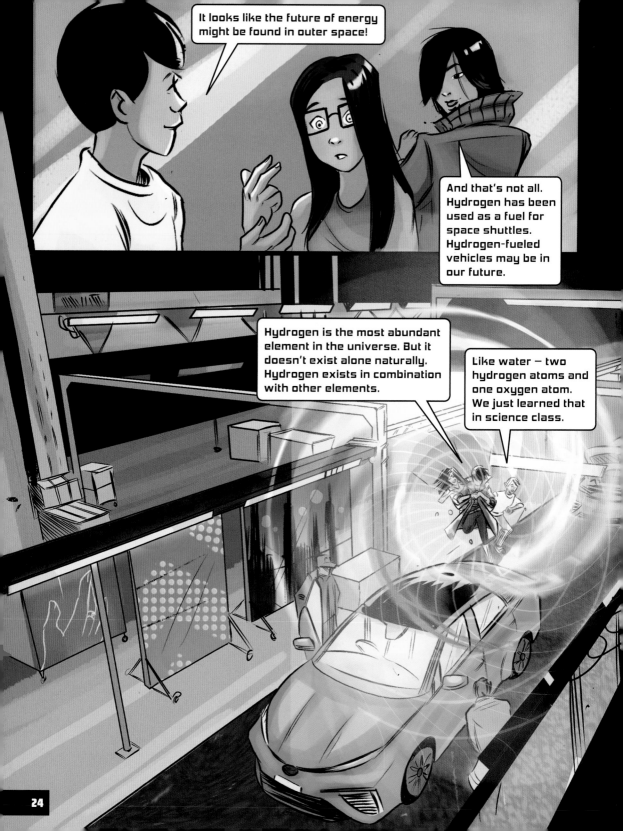

Great! The power is on. Go ahead and plug your phone in, Ken.

12:00

I hope I haven't missed any texts!

Well, did you kids enjoy our little field trip today?

You bet!

How about you, Kami? You seem a little down.

Well, it seems like no matter what kind of energy we use, nothing is 100 percent safe. They all cause some sort of pollution or danger to the environment.

Well, there are trade-offs for everything. That's why it's so important for us to conserve energy wherever we can.

Yeah, I guess.

You know, I can only think of one solution for this problem.

What's that?

I think you're going to have to become a scientist and come up with a better energy solution.

Yeah ... I like that idea a lot.

MORE ABOUT
ENERGY AND THE FUTURE

- In 1859 the first oil well was drilled by Edwin L. Drake in Titusville, Pennsylvania, USA, for the Seneca Oil Company.

- Coal is made mostly of carbon. Impurities, such as sulfur, are found naturally in coal. When coal is burned at power plants, sulfur combines with oxygen. This forms sulfur dioxide. The Environmental Protection Agency limits the amount of sulfur dioxide that power plants can release into the air. Power plants install devices called scrubbers to remove or "scrub" pollutants such as sulfur dioxide from their exhausts.

- In 2015 the total amount of energy *produced* in the United Kingdom can be broken down into the following percentages: natural gas (30%), coal (23%), oil (1%), renewable (25%), nuclear (22%).

- Wave and tidal energy comes from the ocean. A system that includes turbines and buoys harness the power of waves and tides to make clean, renewable energy. In 2014 the United Kingdom developed 27% of all tidal energy and 23% of all wave energy around the world.

- Ocean waves contain kinetic energy, which is energy of motion. One power generator uses the up-and-down wave motion to force air in and out of a chamber. The air movement spins a turbine, generating electricity.

Like wave and tidal energy, wind power uses kinetic energy to generate electricity. The blades on a wind turbine capture engery by spinning in the wind. The spinning blades are connected to an internal generator, which produces the electricity.

Conditions in the UK are well equipped for wind power. Although new, the United Kingdom's wind industry has been steadily growing its onshore and offshore farms. In 2014, 9.5% of the country's electricity came from wind. In 2015, wind power generated 11%.

MORE ABOUT **LUNA LI**

Futurists are scientists who systematically study and explore possibilities about the future of human society and life on Earth. Luna proved herself to be brilliant in this field at a young age. She excelled in STEM subjects and earned her PhD in Alternative Futures from the University of Hawaii at Manoa. Luna invented a gadget she calls the Future Scenario Generator (FSG) that she wears on her wrist. Luna inputs current and predicted data into the FSG. It then crunches the numbers and creates a portal to a holographic reality that humans can enter and interact with.

coal black mineral formed from the remains of ancient plants; coal is mined underground and is burned as a fuel

crude oil thick, black substance drilled from the Earth and used to make fuels such as gasoline and natural gas

fossil fuel natural fuel formed from the remains of plants and animals; coal, oil and natural gas are fossil fuels

generator machine that produces electricity by turning a magnet inside a coil of wire

global warming apparent gradual rise in the temperature of the Earth's atmosphere caused by the greenhouse effect

greenhouse gases gases such as carbon dioxide and methane that are found in the Earth's atmosphere and help hold heat in

power plant building or group of buildings used to create electricity

refinery place where petroleum is made into gasoline, motor oil, and other products

turbine engine powered by steam or gas; the steam or gas moves through the blades of a fanlike device and makes it turn

Brilliant!: Shining a Light on Sustainable Energy (Orca Footprints), Michelle Mulder (Orca Book Publishers, 2013)

Bridging the Energy Gap (The Environment Challenge), Andrew Langley (Raintree, 2012)

How Harmful are Fossil Fuel (Earth Debates), Catherine Chambers (Raintree, 2015)

WEBSITES

http://www.carbonbrief.org/mapped-how-the-uk-generates-its-electricity
Find out how the United Kingdom makes energy.

http://www.bbc.co.uk/schools/gcsebitesize/science/aqa_pre_2011/energy/heatrev4.shtml
Learn about the different types of energy.

http://www.bbc.co.uk/education/guides/znn9q6f/activity
Play a game and learn about renewable energy!